TEACH YOURSELF T

PIANO
SONGS

To access audio visit:
www.halleonard.com/mylibrary

Enter Code
5010-9527-0580-1735

ISBN 978-1-4950-3545-6

HAL•LEONARD®
CORPORATION
7777 W. BLUEMOUND RD. P.O. BOX 13819 MILWAUKEE, WI 53213

Visit Hal Leonard Online at
www.halleonard.com

BOHEMIAN RHAPSODY

One of rock music's most well-known classics, "Bohemian Rhapsody" is lengthy and multi-sectional, highlighting keyboard, guitar, and vocals. For this lesson we'll focus on the opening and the piano ballad section.

Close, intense vocal harmonies originally sung *a capella* mark the beginning of this arrangement. To create a full sound on the piano, the chords are shared between the hands, with both hands starting above middle C, notated with two treble clefs.

Reading four notes at a time can seem like a challenge, but thinking about the notes as **intervals** makes it easy. Intervals are used to describe the distance between two notes in numbers, such as 2nds, 3rds, 4ths, etc. These first four measures are made up almost entirely of 3rds, and a few 4ths. The staff below shows a 3rd, sometimes described as a **skip**, because to play a 3rd you must skip a key, and on the staff, you also skip a line or space. Then, you'll see a 4th, one note larger than a third, and another line or space farther on the staff.

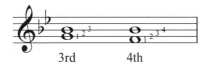

Take a look at the first two measures. All the intervals are 3rds. Find the notes on your piano, using the keyboard diagram as a guide.

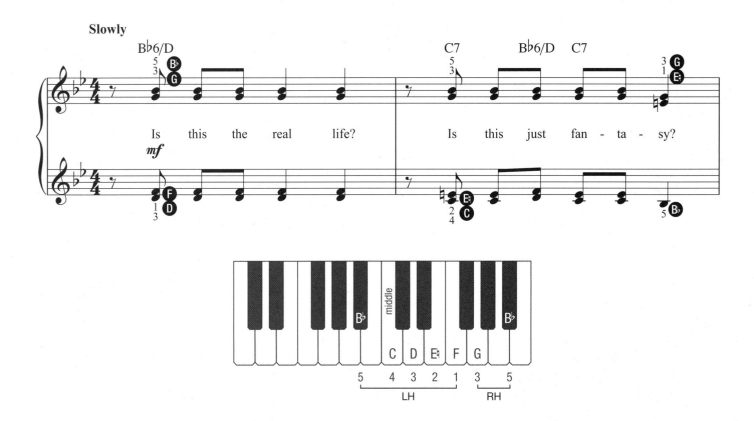

Look at measures 3-4. Both hands are still playing 3rds, shifting slightly up and down the keyboard. Don't be confused by the 5/4 time signature. This just gives measure 3 an extra beat, with 4/4 returning in measure 4. Note that the left hand moves into the bass clef in measure 4, and the right hand plays a 4th in addition to the 3rds.

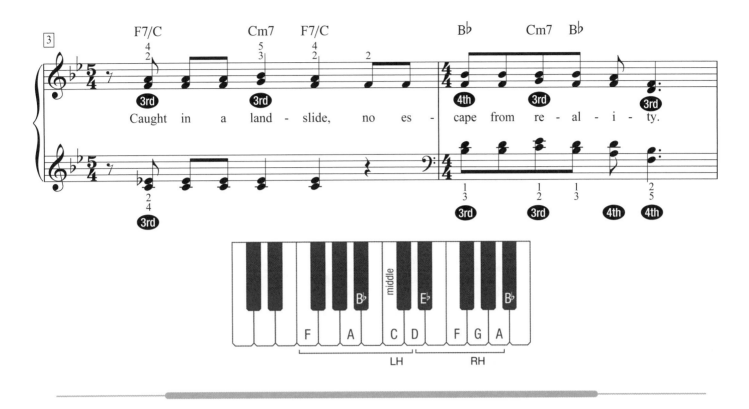

Continue on with measures 5-9. The left hand changes to single notes, while the right hand continues in 3rds and 4ths.

There's a new interval in measure 9, the interval of a 6th. This interval fits very easily in your hand. When playing all five fingers on consecutive keys, move your thumb or your fifth finger to play a 6th. Before playing the next section, look through the next example. All the intervals are labeled for you.

Let's jump ahead to the section that ends this arrangement. Here you'll have a chance to practice reading all the intervals you've already learned. Right and left hand play 2nds, 3rds, 4ths, 5ths, and even 7ths, all labeled for you to study.

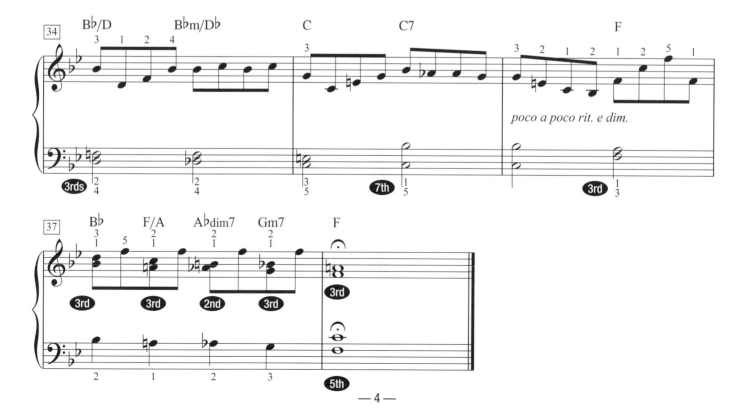

BOHEMIAN RHAPSODY

Words and Music by
FREDDIE MERCURY

COLOUR MY WORLD

This slow and gentle ballad by the rock/jazz fusion group Chicago includes many "colorful" major 7th and 9th chords. You'll recognize this tune from the very first chord, a flowing Fmaj7 that winds through a 12-bar chord progression repeated twice. The opening piano solo deserves a close look at each hand. Once you've tackled the opening section, you'll have the rest of the song under your fingers in no time.

Concentrating on the right hand, divide this opening section into two parts. The first six measures include five different chords, but the right hand plays only three different patterns. The right-hand part is written squarely in the middle of the keyboard, at middle C.

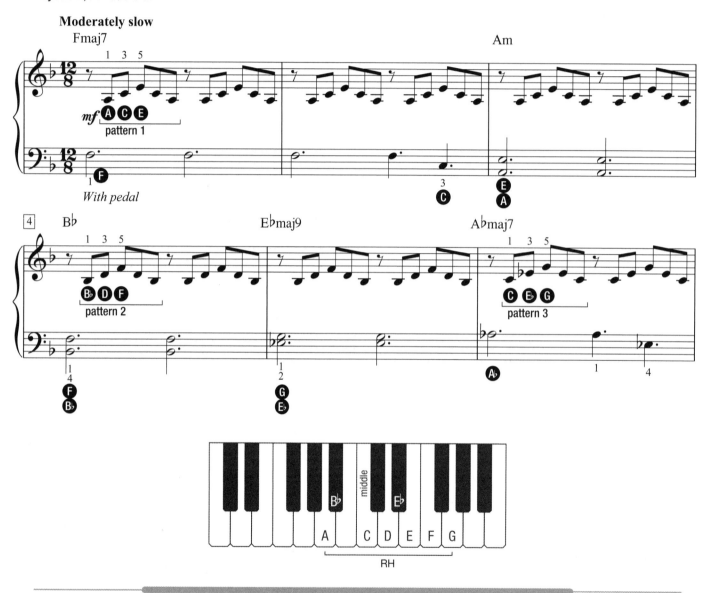

Moving on to measures 7-13, there are three new right-hand patterns to learn. Take your time moving from chord to chord, looking ahead to determine if your hand will shift up or down when the pattern changes.

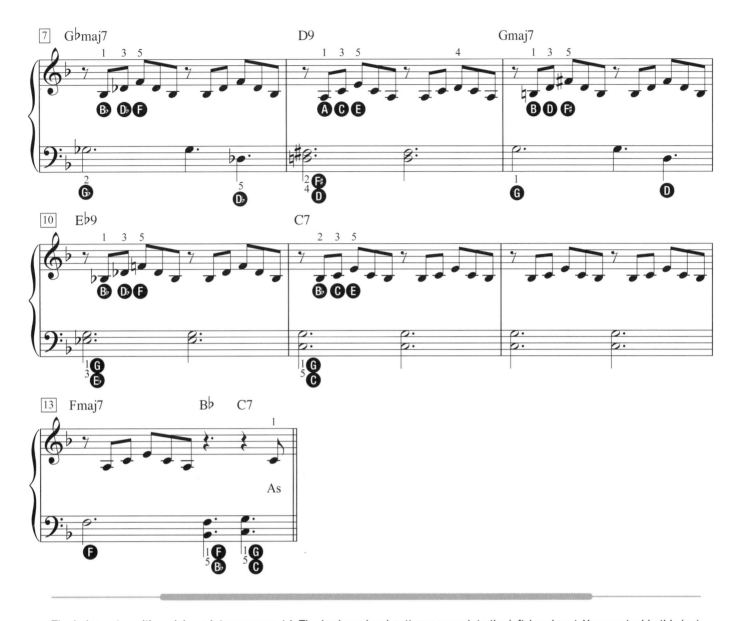

The lyrics enter with a pick-up into measure 14. The broken chord patterns move into the left-hand part. You can tackle this just like the first section. Identify the notes of the chord, and look for changes in the pattern, working with just the left hand alone.

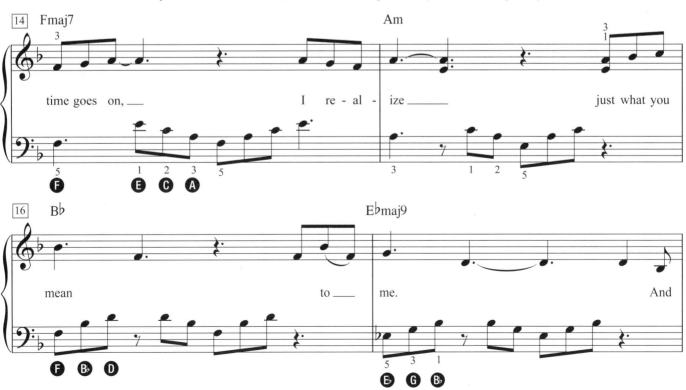

COLOUR MY WORLD

Words and Music by
JAMES PANKOW

Moderately slow

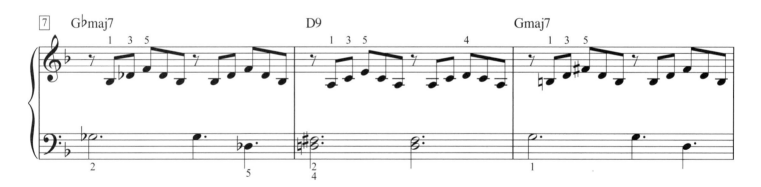

col-our my world _____ with hopes _____ of lov - ing you.

COME SAIL AWAY

Like a music box, both hands will play in the higher part of the keyboard in this introduction. Notice that left-hand notes are placed in the treble clef because they are above middle C. Block each chord before playing the notes as written. Start with the C major chord in measure 1, playing C-E-G together. Now move your hand up a step to the right and block the D minor chord, D-F-A together. Move up another step to the right and block the E minor chord. Then move back to the Dm and C chords. Now, you can easily break up each chord as written in the bottom-top-middle-top-bottom pattern.

Left hand plays in treble clef.

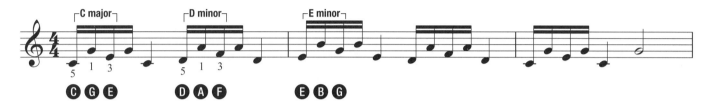

While learning the right hand, be ready to stretch to reach some notes. Follow the finger numbers provided. When you're confident with your right hand, practice measures 1-3 hands together.

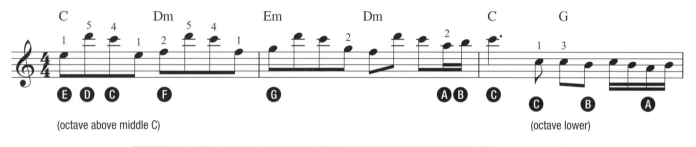

The right hand plays the melody when the lyrics begin at measure 4. Play along with the audio if you need a review. Note the finger numbers given for ease in moving around the keyboard.

Measure 15 really lets loose with the famous guitar chords in a catchy rhythm that continues to the end. Listen to the audio if you need help counting this rhythm. Both hands move lower at this point. Practice right hand first, jumping from treble C to middle C and continuing. Next practice the left-hand jump from middle C to bass C. Notice that the bass Cs repeat while your left thumb moves to create three harmonic changes that repeat to the end.

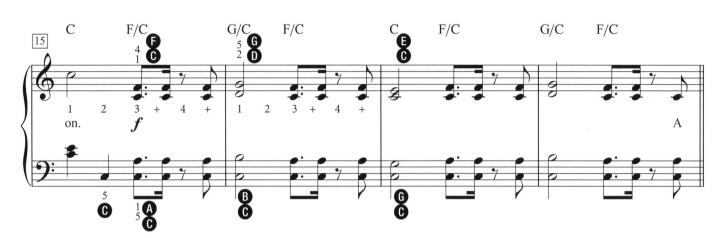

There are only two measures of material to learn on the last page. The syncopated rhythm might look challenging, but listen to the audio for help. Practice the right-hand movement on the lyric "me." It's easy when you see that finger 5 moves to the A that was just played by finger 3. That quick position change sets your hand in place to keep repeating this refrain to the end.

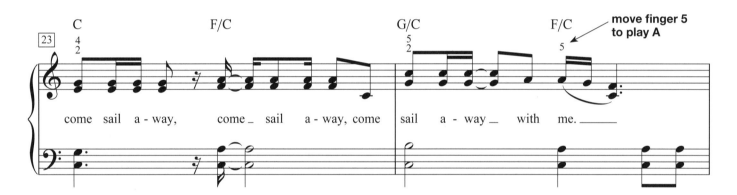

COME SAIL AWAY

Words and Music by
DENNIS DeYOUNG

HOME AT LAST

Swing this funky Steely Dan jazz-rock classic! The bass line is firmly grounded on low G, and the right hand plays 7th chords in close position. Check the fingering for the first Gm7 chord: 5-3-2-1. The chord changes to Dm9 in the next measure. To play the Dm9 chord, move each of the notes one note lower. The fingering suggestion here is slightly different: 5-4-2-1. The chords create a funky accent on beats three and four. Study the counting written in, and be sure to observe the eighth note rests to help achieve this rhythmic emphasis.

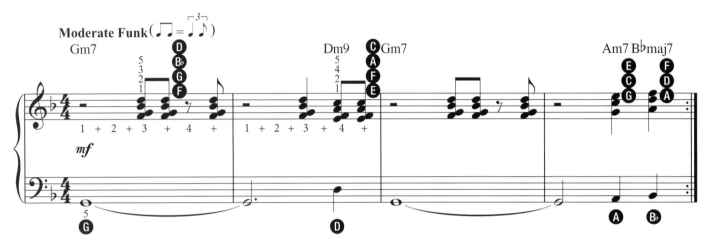

When the melody enters in measure 9, move left-hand finger 5 up to the E♭, sliding your hand closer to the fingerboard. Practice moving from this E♭ to the B♭ in the next measure, which creates the foundation for this section.

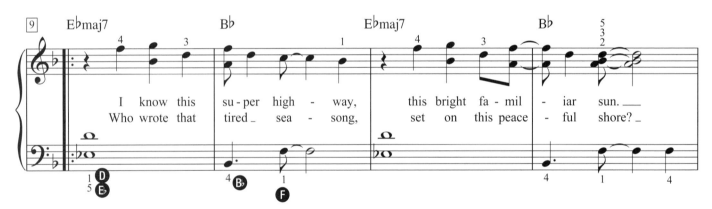

Heading into the chorus you'll hear the Cm7 chord. The bass hangs out with C, G and D played as single notes. Note the fingering in measure 20. Crossing finger 3 over thumb allows you to reach the Gm9 chord in measure 21. Once you've tackled measures 19-22 you'll easily play the rest of the chorus, as those four measures are repeated twice more with just a bit of variation.

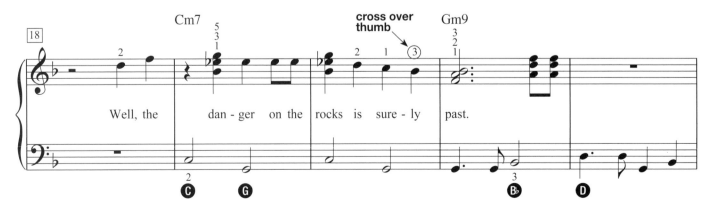

This arrangement ends with another piano solo section very similar to the opening measures. End with a good amount of energy, and aim for the final low note, a G one octave lower than the low G you've been playing.

HOME AT LAST

Words and Music by WALTER BECKER
and DONALD FAGEN

Home at last.

IT'S TOO LATE

Carole King loves the middle range of the keyboard in this chart-topping hit. Once you've learned the verse and chorus, you'll be able to jam on the whole tune. Right off the bat you'll notice right and left hands play close together, with bass and chords spanning only about an octave and a half. You're positioned right around middle C, making it easy to get your bearings. Let's take a look at the introduction.

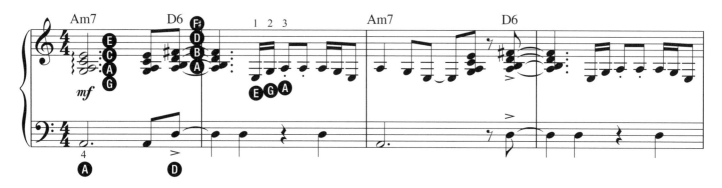

Don't be fooled by all the ledger lines in the right hand. Although these can look hard to read, they are not. Middle C is the closest ledger line to the staff. These ledger lines are used to notate the notes that fall right in between the bass and treble staff. The left hand alternates between Am7 and D6, firmly establishing the minor feel with a jazzy twist.

Moving into the verse, you'll play a syncopated rhythm followed by the melodic motif you learned in the introduction.

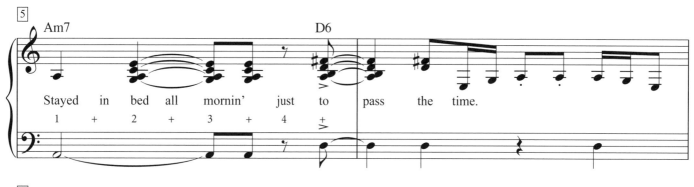

Building on the Am7 and D6, Gm7 and Fmaj7 chords lead into the chorus. The left-hand bass notes are the same as the chords named above the treble staff.

Repeated chords in the right hand continue through the chorus. Be sure to take some time counting through the syncopated rhythms until they're second nature. Use the online audio to help lock these in place, or if you just need a quick review.

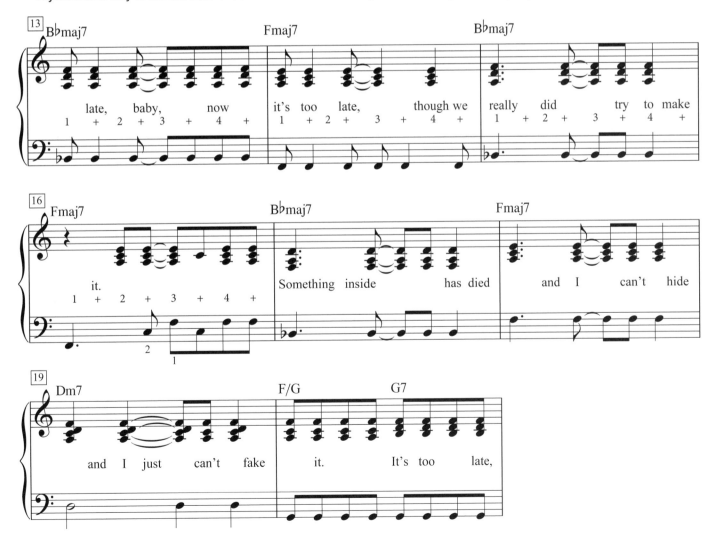

IT'S TOO LATE

Words and Music by CAROLE KING
and TONI STERN

Stayed in bed all mornin' just to pass the time.

There's something wrong here, there can be no denyin'.

One of us is changin', or maybe we've just stopped tryin'.

JUMP

You'll recognize the driving synth line of this Van Halen classic right away, but if you're unfamiliar with this song, listen to the online audio to get a sense of the syncopated chord stabs. Begin by learning the first four measures. Once you're comfortable with this material, it'll be easy to move ahead.

Take some time to identify and find the chords on the keyboard. Practice moving from chord to chord. Now play the chords in rhythm. We've written in the counting, and you can also listen and play along with the online audio. Left hand begins on the low C, two octaves below middle C.

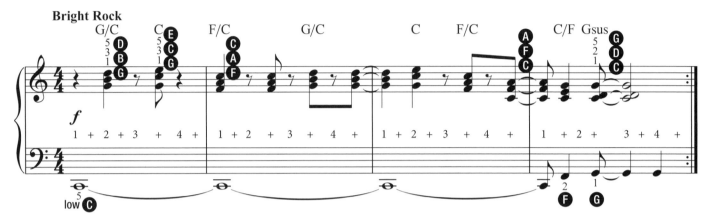

The first four measures repeat, and the next four measures are exactly the same, except the left hand plays repeated eighth notes on the low C. In measures 9-12 the right hand shifts an octave higher for two measures before returning to the middle of the keyboard.

The verse begins with a pick-up into measure 13. Left hand continues with a simple bass-note part, and the right hand incorporates short melodic phrases around the chord stabs you learned previously. It might take a bit of practice to "jump" between the two musical ideas here, but you'll quickly master this with a little practice.

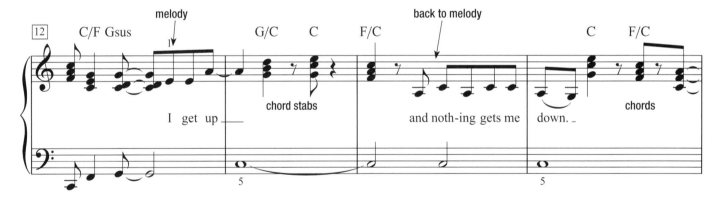

The bridge (measures 29-35) offers a contrast with a break from the right-hand chords, a simpler melody line, and the addition of Am and Dm chords.

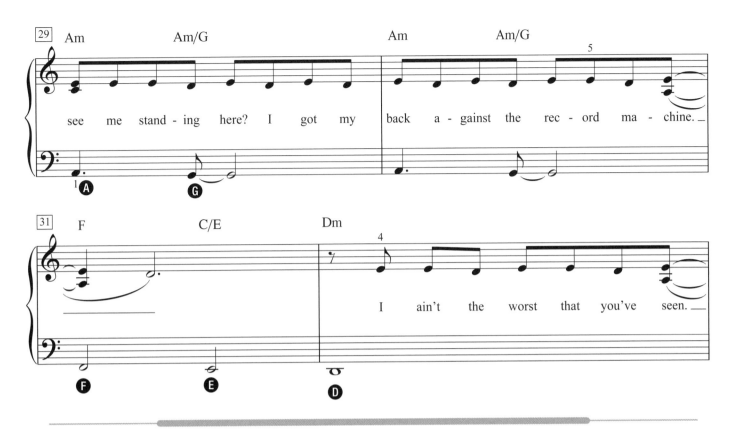

Familiar material returns at the chorus, with short melodic phrases again alternating with the same syncopated chords.
Drive straight through the chorus, ending with one final blast of synthesizer solo.

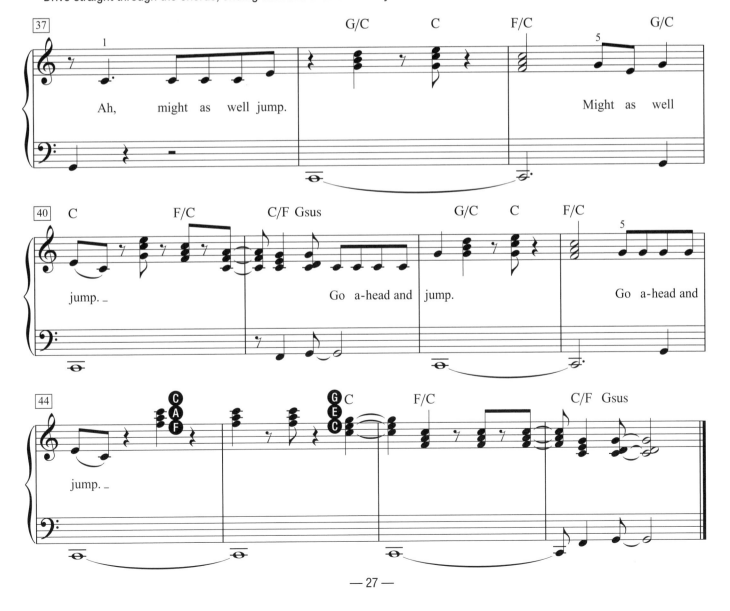

JUMP

Words and Music by EDWARD VAN HALEN,
ALEX VAN HALEN and DAVID LEE ROTH

MY LIFE

Billy Joel's classic rock hit "My Life" opens with an iconic keyboard riff. In the original version this riff returns between verse and chorus, and again at the end of the song. The driving left-hand octaves give this song its signature sound and high energy feel. They're also very fun to play.

A quick look through the arrangement here will show the left hand playing alternating octave notes throughout. This makes the left-hand part easy to learn. It takes a bit of stamina to keep the octaves going, but with practice you'll master this technique. Here are a few things to keep in mind as you work on the left hand.

- Keep your hand and fingers loose as you rotate between the octave notes.
- The rotating motion is much like the motion you need to turn a doorknob-it's all in the wrist, not the arm.
- If your hand starts to tire, or feel stiff, stop and shake out your hand and arm.
- If you want to play hands together, but need to concentrate on the right hand, let your left hand relax a bit by playing only the lowest note of the octave as quarter notes.
- Play short sections at a time as you build up your ability to play the octaves at the tempo needed.

Let's dive right into the octaves. For the first eight measures, your left hand alternates between octave Ds. Check out the keyboard diagram, and play the opening measures with a relaxed, easy feel.

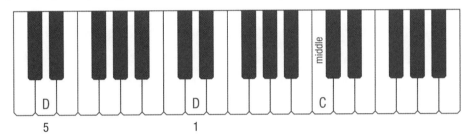

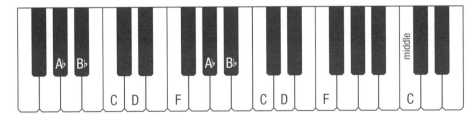

In measures 9-16 the octaves change, creating a bit of movement for your left hand. You'll be playing octaves with D-C-F. In measure 12 you'll have some fun with a bit of chromatic motion, moving down in half steps, (black key-white key-black key) B♭-A-A♭.

Measures 12-16 are the same, except in measure 16 the chromatic octaves move up: B♭-C-C♯.

The right hand enters in measure 4, playing a pattern of 6ths. The pattern repeats twice more, with a variation the third time.

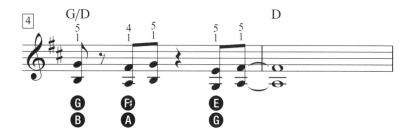

Once you're comfortable with the right-hand part this far, take a look at measures 9-16. In addition to 6ths, you'll add 3rds and 2nds. Keep an eye out for the syncopated rhythm on the high G in measure 14. Listen to the audio if you are uncertain of how that fits in.

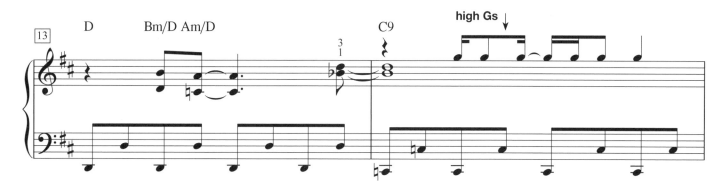

The vocals enter in measure 17, continuing with familiar 6ths in the right hand and left-hand octaves. Billy Joel really explores the lower register of the piano here. In measure 18 you'll need to jump way down to the low F, two octaves below middle C, and stay in that range for the next few measures.

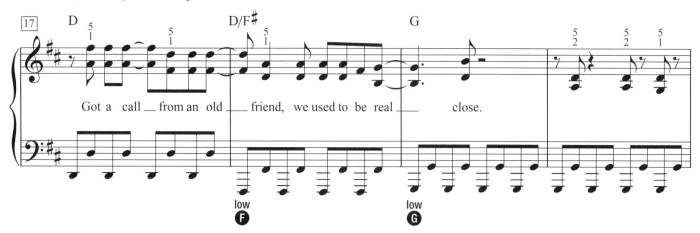

You can easily divide this vocal section in half. Each half is similar, and you'll recognize material you've already learned in earlier measures. As you continue to practice and work on your octave technique, take things slowly at first, and use the features on the audio (left hand alone, right hand alone, slower tempos, etc.) to help you.

MY LIFE

Words and Music by
BILLY JOEL

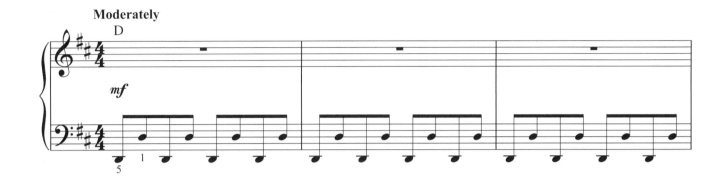

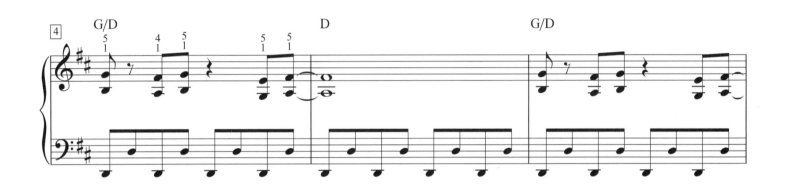

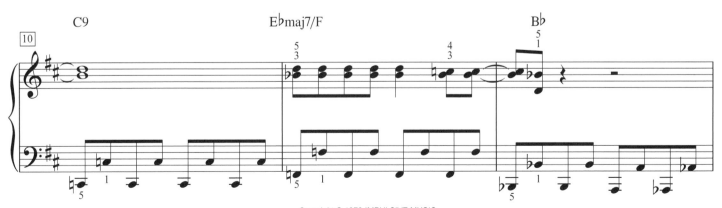

Coast.

Now he gives them a stand-

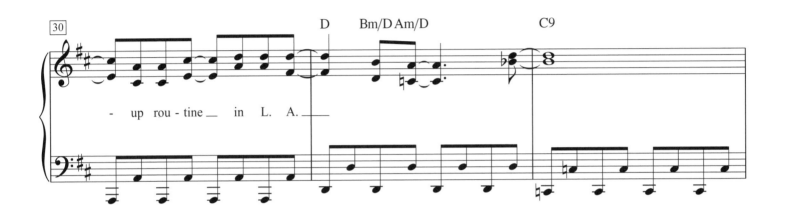

up rou-tine in L. A.

Keep it to your-self, it's my life.

NOVEMBER RAIN

Guns N' Roses gives us a lengthy symphonic ballad filled with vocals, guitar solos, and a pensive piano opening, which we will focus on here. The piano chords continue throughout the original, giving the tune forward motion and a steady rhythmic sensibility.

From the very first note, the piano gets things started. Take a look at the first measure. The left hand plays octave Fs, with the lowest F two full octaves below middle C. The right hand has a grace note E heading into the F half note. Play the grace note quickly, just ever so slightly before beat 3. Notice how this opening measure covers four octaves of the keyboard, really pointing up the piano's wide range.

The opening uses only four chords: F, C, Am, and Dm. You're in the lower range of the keyboard here, but it's easy to know which notes to play. Just check the chord labels above the treble staff if you are unsure. With only four notes bass to choose from, you'll memorize these octaves in no time at all.

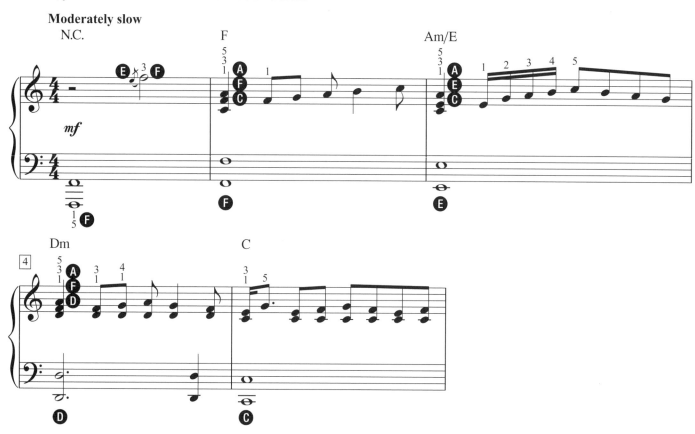

Almost every measure begins with a right-hand chord, followed by the notes of the chord, sometimes with passing notes added. If you take some time to study each measure, you'll see that your hand never moves outside the interval of an octave, and there are lots of repeated notes to help you find your way. Within each measure, all the notes are pretty close together. We've highlighted some examples here.

Chords with passing notes:

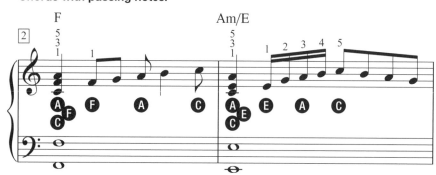

bottom note of chord repeats:

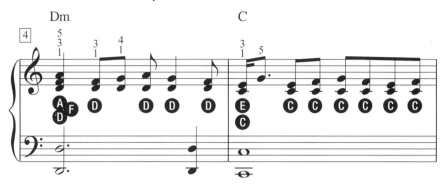

Look ahead to measure 16. The right hand changes to repeated chords, and the left-hand octaves play some interesting syncopation. To get the feel for this, listen to the audio, and take a look at the example below to see exactly where the eighth notes fit in. The chords change just a bit here too. Fmaj7 is an F chord with an added E. Dm9 is D minor with an added E. So, the only thing that changes when moving between these chords is the bass note!

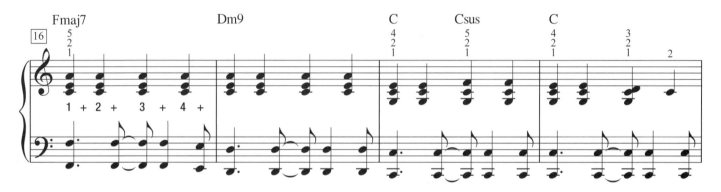

A new progression, Fmaj7-Dm9-C-Csus-C leads us into the first vocal entrance. Now our arrangement puts both chords and bass note in the left hand, freeing up the right hand to play the melody. Listen, and sing along with the melody, and when ready, add the left hand chords. If you are playing with a vocalist, you might choose to double the chords with the right hand, instead of playing the melody.

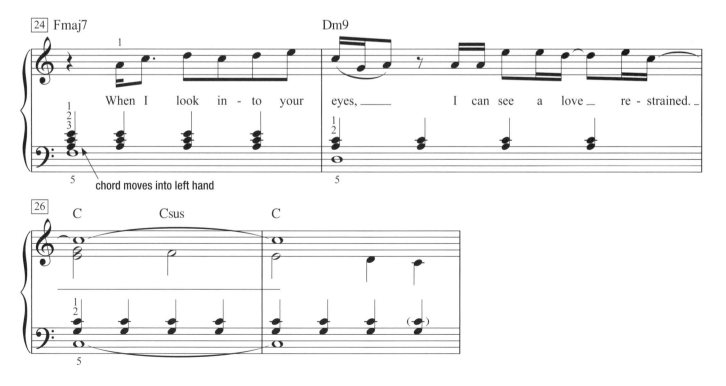

NOVEMBER RAIN

Words and Music by
W. AXL ROSE

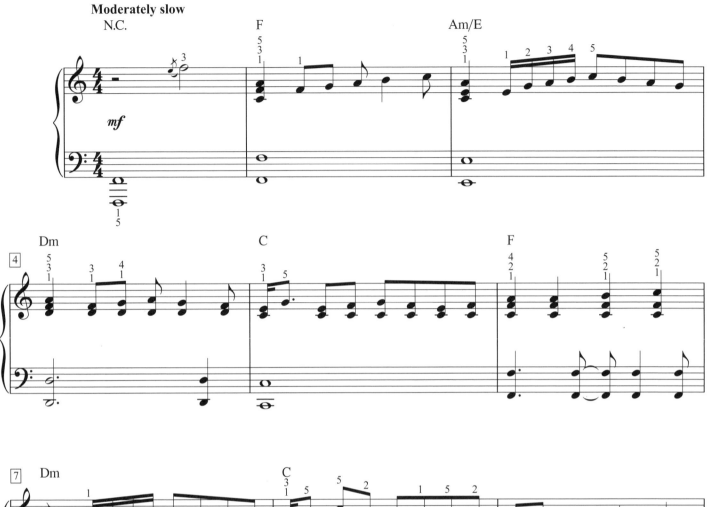

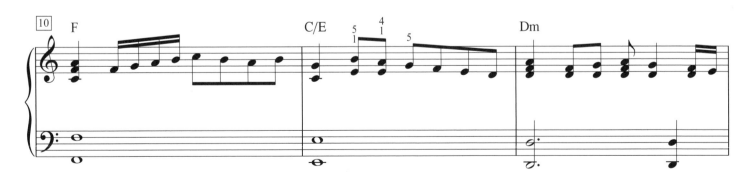

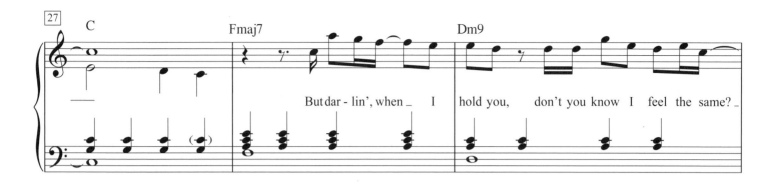

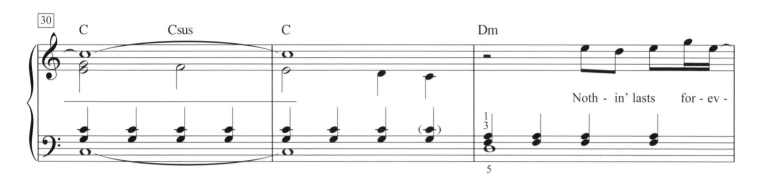

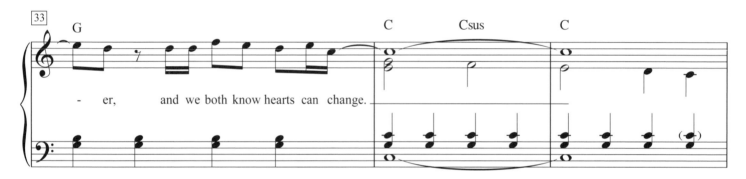

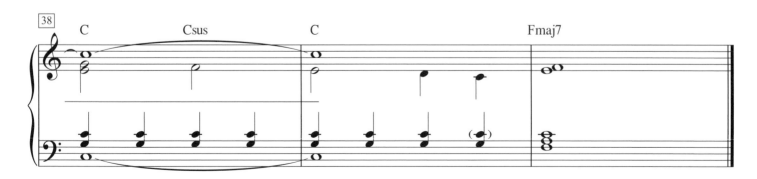

WEREWOLVES OF LONDON

Zevon's cool piano riff is simply constructed and fun to play. The entire song is created with two measures and only three chords. Let's jump right in!

Looking at the right-hand part, you can see that the notes are close together, and pretty much stay in one place. All the notes you need to play fit within an octave, with the lowest note being middle C.

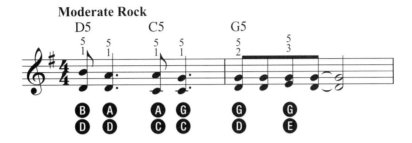

You're probably familiar with the syncopation that gives this riff its identity, the quick eighth followed by the dotted quarter note. Play the eighth note lightly, with a bit of spring, so you can land with energy on the dotted note. If you need to review this rhythm, listen to the online audio.

Memorize these right-hand measures. Now you've learned the entire right-hand part, and can turn your attention to the left hand.

The first thing you'll notice about the left hand is the ledger lines extending below the staff. Don't let those low notes slow you down. If you identify the notes written within the bass clef staff, you'll see that the lower notes are just an octave below. Practice slowly at first, memorizing as you go.

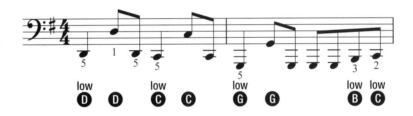

Play slowly the first few times you try hands together. If you're comfortable playing each hand alone it won't take long to line up the right-hand chords with the left-hand notes. Memorize your two-measure pattern, so you can sing along with the lyrics when they enter at measure 4.

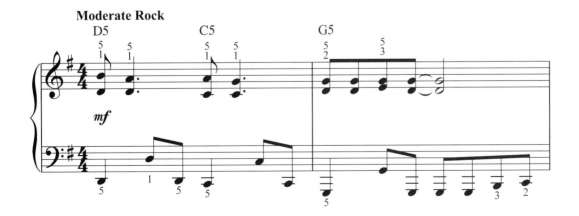

WEREWOLVES OF LONDON

Words and Music by WARREN ZEVON,
WADDY WACHTEL and LEROY MARINELL

I saw a werewolf with a Chinese
You hear him howlin' around your

menu in his hand.
kitchen door. _

walking through the streets of Soho
You better not let him in!

in the rain.

He was looking for a place called
Little old lady got mutilated

SWEET HOME ALABAMA

It's easy to see how Billy Powell's piano gave this iconic Lynryd Skynyd favorite its sparkle! Created with only three chords and a rhythmic drive that's hard to forget, let's jump right in and learn the nuts and bolts of this famous Southern rock song.

The first thing you'll want to focus on is the chord progression D-C-G. Not only does this progression define the song, it outlines where you'll play on the keyboard and uses the rhythm that gives this song its distinctive groove. Almost everything you need to know can be found in the first two measures.

Notice that the right-hand chords are arranged within the span of a 6th, that is, the distance between the top and bottom notes is a 6th, with another note in between. The top note of each chord is the name of the chord.

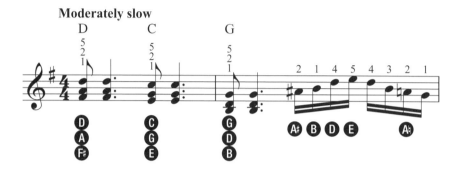

Are you familiar with the distinctive rhythm of this song? The eighth note followed by dotted quarter note (sounds like, "short-long, short-long, short-long") is one of the most identifiable parts of the song. If you're unsure of how this sounds, listen to the online audio for a review.

Now let's add the left hand. The bottom note of each fifth matches the name of the chord, making those notes easy to find. And, as in the right hand, the move from D-C is very close, just one note lower, while the move from C to G is a little bit of a leap. Check out the left-hand notes labeled for you below.

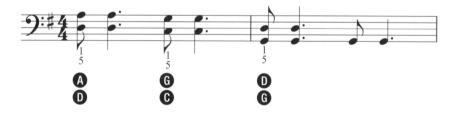

At the end of the second measure, the right hand plays a nifty little 16th-note riff. It fits easily under your hand once you know which notes to play and which fingers to use. Play slowly at first, speeding up as you feel comfortable. You might even want to memorize this little bit, since it's repeated frequently throughout the song.

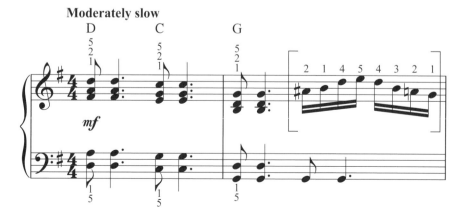

— 44 —

A quick look at the left-hand once the vocals start will show you that the left hand continues with the same rhythm and notes you played in the introduction. The chord progression remains the same; the only difference is that you're playing just the bass notes, not fifths.

The right hand plays the melody, so sing along as you learn the right-hand part. There's one more nifty riff to learn in the right hand, at the end of measure 8.

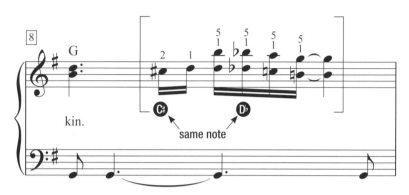

If you study the example above, you'll see how following the fingering helps propel you up to the high notes you need, and that moving in 6ths is easy—just move down by half steps playing the 6th with fingers 5-1 each time. Once you know the notes, it almost feels like you're sliding down the keys here. As you continue through the music on your own, you'll be able to recognize how cleverly the rest of the song is woven out of the elements you've already learned. This arrangement concludes with a short instrumental ending using material from the introduction.

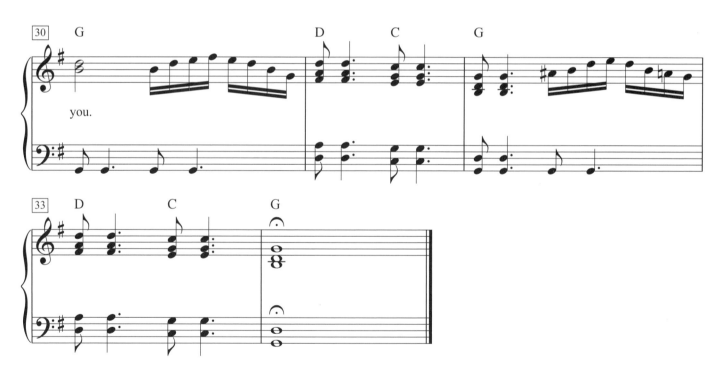

SWEET HOME ALABAMA

Words and Music by RONNIE VAN ZANT,
ED KING and GARY ROSSINGTON

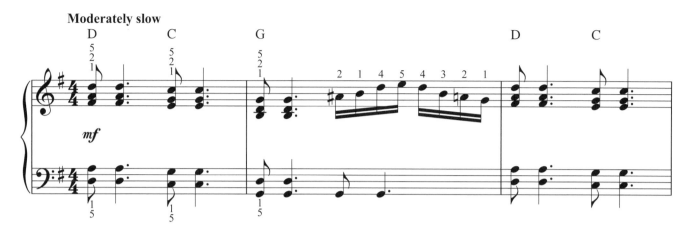

Big wheels keep on

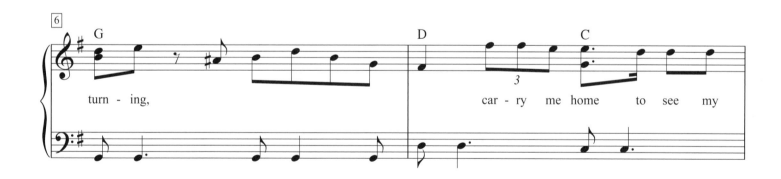

turn - ing,   car - ry me home to see my

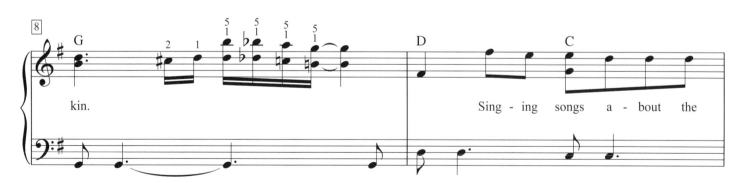

kin.   Sing - ing songs a - bout the